Pay for College

using the

Internet and
Social Media

Marianne Ragins

TSW Publishing
P. O. Box 176
Centreville, Virginia 20122
www.scholarshipworkshop.com
TSW Publishing is a division of The Scholarship Workshop LLC

Pay for College Using the Internet and Social Media was written to provide accurate advice to readers. However, please note that the author nor the publisher are engaged in the practice of providing legal, accounting, tax or other professional advice unless otherwise indicated. If you need legal, accounting, tax or other advice, please consult a professional in the appropriate area. Neither the author, the publisher, nor any entity associated with *Pay for College Using the Internet and Social Media* assume any liability for errors, omissions, or inaccuracies. Any action you take or do not take as a result of reading *Pay for College Using the Internet and Social Media* is entirely your responsibility.

ISBN: 978-1-950653-03-4

Printed in the United States of America

This book is available at special quantity discounts for bulk purchases for sales promotions, premiums, fundraising, and educational use. Special versions or book excerpts can also be created to fit specific needs.

For more information, please contact
info@scholarshipworkshop.com or call 703 579-4245. You can also write: TSW Publishing, P. O. Box 176, Centreville, Virginia 20122.

Dedication

To my mother, my husband, and my little ones—your love, motivation, and presence in my life keep me going.

To Aria and Cameron — your input and suggestions were greatly appreciated.

For Gloria Laverne Solomon, Sammie L. Moore Sr. and Dr. Angela E. Grant
As people who truly got the most from life
and helped us to get the most from ours,
your sunny smiles, loving hearts and
generous ways will be remembered forever
by all of your family and friends.

Contents

Introduction

When it comes to research, the Internet is a giant library of information especially when researching college and scholarship information. The Internet has a major advantage over traditional types of paper based communication because web pages can be instantly updated by organizations and educational institutions. Organizations can update their web pages more frequently and less expensively than a book, directory, or catalog, thus giving them the ability to provide more accurate, up-to-date, and thorough information. In fact, most colleges and universities use their web pages to attract students. On their web sites, many have realistic images of almost every area of their institution, and allow you to take virtual campus tours.

Using the Internet you can:

- Connect to college web pages and take virtual campus tours in your own home.
- Perform extensive scholarship searches using free computerized databases and search engines.
- Visit scholarship program web sites such as the Coca-Cola Scholars Foundation to find out more information. With many scholarship programs such as the Coca-Cola Scholars Foundation, you can even apply online.
- Visit organizations such as the National Association of Secondary School Principals that administer or sponsor scholarships to

find out more about them and how to win scholarships they sponsor or administer.

- Read financial aid information from a variety of sources, including the U.S. Department of Education
- Take practice standardized tests such as the SAT or view sample questions and tips from the SAT.
- Talk to college students and scholarship program administrators by sending e-mail, chatting online or using social media.
- Submit college applications, financial aid applications such as the Free Application for Federal Student Aid (FAFSA), and other types of applications online.

An online college and scholarship search can save you a lot of time and can usually be done more quickly and easily than a paper-based search. When I began my scholarship search in the early nineties, I spent a lot of time in the library poring over directories for several weeks. My advice for you, now that we have technology to make things easier, is to use the Internet as a way to make your search as comprehensive as possible. This way you will miss out on very few of the scholarship dollars you are eligible to win. One of the main reasons students do not apply for scholarships is that they don't know what is available in scholarship money. One of my primary goals for this book and the workshops I conduct is to help you find scholarships no matter where you live or your personal eligibility criteria. Once you find them, my next goal is to show you how to win them. This is why I caution that if you do research online, you should not skip any of the research methods discussed in this publication and *Winning Scholarships for College.* The Internet does not have all of the information about scholarships to be found nor is all the information you find accurate. This means that you should still look at all the current paper based scholarship directories and periodicals you can find and conduct local research. Also, you should still call local organizations, banks, television stations, and radio stations. Much of the information on the Internet is from large or nationally oriented scholarship programs. If you rely on the Internet exclusively, or even scholarship directories whose focus is also national, you could miss out on local opportunities closer to home. You should also note that while doing your research online, particularly for scholarships and financial aid, that not every web site has legitimate information or scholarships.

Following are the most popular and frequently used directories, databases, and search engines on the Internet. Using them, you can obtain a comprehensive listing of scholarship sources and information for college.

General Search Engines

- Google (www.google.com)
- Yahoo! (www.yahoo.com)
- Bing (www.bing.com)
- AOL Search (http://search.aol.com)
- Ask! (www.ask.com)
- Excite (www.excite.com)
- WebCrawler (www.webcrawler.com)

When you use these search engines to find

scholarships and financial aid information, you should use keywords such as "financial aid," "scholarships," "college scholarships," "money for college," "education," "college aid," "grants," "fellowships," "pay for college," "paying for college," "scholarship applications," "merit scholarships," "academic scholarships," "minority scholarships," and so on. Make sure to use quotation marks around your entries to get the most relevant results information. You can also conduct an advanced search explained later in this publication.

General search engines can also help you find scholarships based on special events or holidays. For example, I have found scholarships for Mother's Day, Father's Day, and the Martin Luther King Jr. holiday. Think of the next upcoming holiday or a major national event and use a search engine to determine if there is an available scholarship with an upcoming deadline you can meet.

Use free search engines that focus primarily on scholarships. I call them computerized scholarship search services. Some of the most popular are listed in this publication. Consider linking to these free searches by visiting www.scholarshipworkshop.com.

Search for major companies and associations and explore their web sites to see if they sponsor scholarship programs. When searching company home pages, you should use their search function and type "scholarships" in the keyword search box. If this doesn't yield results, consider visiting sections of their web sites that may be labeled as *About Us*, *Philanthropy*, *Corporate Giving*, or *Foundation*. You can also do this for associations. For example, in a search of the National Association of Secondary School Principals, you would find information on scholarship programs and awards which they administer or for which they provide information. To find more associations, consult the *Encyclopedia of Associations* or *The Foundation Directory* to get the names of other organizations and associations to search for on the Internet. Both directories can be usually found in the local library in a print and/or electronic version.

You could also conduct an advanced Internet search such as the following to find a specific organization or association.

Advanced Search		
Find Results	all of these words	association
	the exact phrase	scholarship
	any of these words	journalists
	none of these words	

When you find associations, you can search their web sites for possible scholarships they may have available. Associations and organizations of professionals in your area of study can be scholarship and financial aid gold mines!

To find associations and organizations in your area of study and check to see if any of them offer scholarships, look at the previously mentioned *Encyclopedia of Associations* published by Gale Re-search. Or use an advanced Internet search also mentioned previously. When I did this, I found the National Society of Professional Engineers (NSPE) web site as well as many others. I went to the NSPE web site and used their site search engine to search for scholarships. Using this method I found a Paul H. Robbins, P.E., Honorary Scholarship for undergraduate students.

Review web search portals such as Google and others listed in this publication to search for organizations in your field. I conducted an advanced Internet search for accounting societies and associations and found quite a few that offer scholarships. In the area of accounting, there were at least five organizations offering scholarships; National Society of Accountants, the American Institute of Certified Public Accountants, the American Accounting Association (AAA), the Institute of Management Accountants, and the American Society of Women Accountants. All of these organizations offered some type of accounting scholarship to students.

Be aware that membership can definitely have its privileges. Some associations may require that you are a member of their organization to be eligible for a scholarship. Many others do not. For those that do require you to be a member, the membership fee may be a smaller or reduced amount for students.

Consult *College Survival & Success Skills 101* to review dozens of societies and associations related to various fields of study and interest. Many of them may have scholarship opportunities for you.

Also, to find organizations on the Internet when you do not know their web site address or if they even have a site, you can go to any of the major search engines such as Google or Yahoo! In the search box, type the name of the organization and put quotation marks around it. If the organization is on the web, the search should return an entry for it.

1

Using Scholarship Search Engines and Social Media

For a complete scholarship search on the Internet, start by using all of these free scholarship search services. Exploring all of them is very important since some search engines list scholarships that others may not. Some may even have scholarships created specifically for their website.

- **College Board Scholarship Search -**
  - https://bigfuture.collegeboard.org/scholarship-search
- **Fastweb**
  - www.fastweb.com
- **Mach25 from CollegeNET**
  - www.collegenet.com/mach25
- **Scholarships.com**
  - www.scholarships.com
- **UNCF Scholarship Search**
  - www.uncf.org
- **Scholarship Search by Sallie Mae**
  - www.salliemae.com/plan-for-college/scholarships/scholarship-search
- **Cappex.com**
  - www.cappex.com (*see Scholarships*)
- **Chegg.com**
  - www.chegg.com (*see Scholarships*)

Using Social Media

Increasingly, many organizations use Facebook pages, Twitter handles, YouTube videos, and other forms of social media to assist students with their college and college-funding search. If you want to determine if a program has a social media presence, use the search toolbar in Facebook (http://www.facebook.com) to determine if a Facebook page is available. Just type in the name and see what comes up. YouTube (http://www.youtube.com) has a similar search toolbar to find a program. For Twitter (http://www.twitter.com), use Google and type in the program name along with the name, Twitter, to see if there is a handle for the program. When you review the listing of scholarship programs on the Internet later in this chapter, you see Twitter handles, Facebook pages, and YouTube channels listed as well. In some cases, the social media outlet may not directly relate to the scholarship program, so it was not included, or it may not have been available at the time of publication.

To get you started with Twitter, use these Twitter handles for sites that are helpful to students in search of college aid and college-related information:

@Scholarshipscom
@ScholAmerica
@FAFSA
@CollegeBoard
@CollegeNET
@Unigo

How Can Facebook, Twitter, YouTube, and Other Social Media Help You?

Thorough research of a scholarship foundation, national foundation, or scholarship program can help you prepare to write scholarship essays, perfect your application, and get ready for interviews. If you have prior information about a program it could help you highlight certain personal qualities or activities you've been involved in that could sway the opinions of a scholarship committee in your favor. Students who have no knowledge of a program or a competition will have a tough time winning. Social media can help you keep a finger on the pulse of a program by keeping you aware of the events and news it considered important enough to broadcast on its social media platforms. Specifically, social media can help you in the following ways:

- If you "Like" certain pages for scholarship and college-related programs on Facebook, you may get alerts on scholarship application availability, deadlines, tips, and more.
- Following programs on Twitter can keep you aware of tips, deadline extensions, application availability, and announcements.
- Viewing YouTube videos can help you understand a program's mission, values, and goals, which can help you prepare for an essay or interview. Or, in the case of a competition, you may be able to view previous performances or submissions to help you prepare and perfect your own.

Start Your Internet and Social Media Search with These Scholarship Funding and College Information Sources

To launch your scholarship search on the Internet, use the following listings to get more information about colleges, scholarships and financial aid, and other related advice. Please note that website links and programs change frequently. The list below is meant to give you a starting point with your Internet and social media research. Do not rely solely on this list and do not become frustrated if some of these sites are no longer available. Also, programs can and do stop awarding scholarships or suspend their scholarship programs. Don't get discouraged. You can still find available scholarships. But please know that there are no guarantees about the availability of a given scholarship, or that you will win it. It is important to do your own research, which I outline how to do throughout this book. For up-to-date listings with examples of available scholarships, visit http://www.scholarshipworkshop.com for new and updated listings since the publication of this book. You can also read *10 Steps for Using the Internet in Your Scholarship Search* or *The Scholarship Monthly Planner.* Both publications are updated frequently. Visit http://www.scholarshipworkshop.com for more information.

GOVERNMENT FUNDING, INFORMATION WEBSITES, AND SOCIAL MEDIA

Federal Student Aid and Free Application for Federal Student Aid (FAFSA)

http://www.fafsa.ed.gov or www.fafsa4caster.ed.gov
Facebook:
https://www.facebook.com/FederalStudentAid
Twitter: @FAFSA
YouTube:
http://www.youtube.com/user/federalStudentAid

The Student Guide
http://studentaid.gov or
http://studentaid.ed.gov/resources#funding

IRS Tax Information and Benefits for Students
http://www.irs.gov/Individuals/Students

TEST REGISTRATION AND TEST PREPARATION WEBSITES AND SOCIAL MEDIA

Practice Test Questions for the ACT
http://www.act.org or http://www.actstudent.org
Facebook: https://www.facebook.com/theacttest
Twitter: @ACTStudent

Preparing for the SAT
http://www.collegeboard.com or
https://collegereadiness.collegeboard.org/sat/practice
http://socialmedia.collegeboard.org

Daily SAT Practice App
https://collegereadiness.collegeboard.org/sat/practice/daily-practice-app
Facebook:
https://www.facebook.com/thecollegeboard
Twitter: @CollegeBoard

YouTube: http://www.youtube.com/collegeboard

APPS FOR HELPING YOU FIND SCHOLARSHIPS

Scholly*
https://myscholly.com
Twitter: @MyScholly
Facebook: https://www.facebook.com/MyScholly/
*While most of the services in this chapter are free to use, this app does have a fee.

COLLEGE PREPARATION AND SELECTION

The College Board
http://www.collegeboard.com
http://socialmedia.collegeboard.org
Facebook:
https://www.facebook.com/thecollegeboard
Twitter: @CollegeBoard
YouTube: http://www.youtube.com/collegeboard

Princeton Review
http://www.princetonreview.com
Facebook:
https://www.facebook.com/ThePrincetonReview
Twitter: @ThePrincetonRev
YouTube:
http://www.youtube.com/user/ThePrincetonReviewUS

CollegeNET
http://www.collegenet.com
Facebook: http://www.facebook.com/CollegeNET
Twitter: @CollegeNET

US News Online: Education
http://www.usnews.com (click on Education)

Campus Tours
http://www.campustours.com

College Express
http://www.collegexpress.com
Twitter: @CollegeXpress

ALTERNATIVE EDUCATION RESOURCES

Distance Education Accrediting Commission (DEAC)
https://www.deac.org

MAJOR SCHOLARSHIP AND COLLEGE INFORMATION SITES: INTERNET AND SOCIAL MEDIA REFERENCES

The College Board
http://www.collegeboard.com
http://socialmedia.collegeboard.org
Facebook:
https://www.facebook.com/thecollegeboard
Twitter: @CollegeBoard
YouTube: http://www.youtube.com/collegeboard

The Scholarship Workshop Online
https://www.scholarshipworkshop.com
Facebook:
https://www.facebook.com/scholarshipworkshop

Twitter: @ScholarshipWork

FinAid!—The SmartStudent Guide to Financial Aid
http://www.finaid.org

Peterson's Education Center
http://www.petersons.com
Facebook: https://www.facebook.com/petersons
Twitter: @Petersons

RaiseMe
https://www.raise.me
Facebook: https://www.facebook.com/RaiseLabs
Twitter:https://twitter.com/raiselabs

CORPORATE/ORGANIZATION
SCHOLARSHIP AND AWARD WEBSITES

Coca-Cola Scholars Foundation
http://www.coca-colascholars.org
Facebook: https://www.facebook.com/cokescholars
Twitter: @cokescholars
YouTube:
http://www.youtube.com/user/CocaColaScholars/fe
ed

Veterans of Foreign Wars of the United States
http://www.vfw.org (click on
Community\YouthandEducation\Youth
Scholarships)

National YoungArts Foundation
http://www.youngarts.org

Facebook:
https://www.facebook.com/YoungArtsFoundation
Twitter: @YoungArts
YouTube:
https://www.youtube.com/user/YoungArtsNFAA

Regeneron Science Talent Search
https://student.societyforscience.org/regeneron-sts
Facebook:
https://www.facebook.com/societyforscience
YouTube:
http://www.youtube.com/societyforscience

The Ayn Rand Institute
http://www.aynrand.org/contests
Facebook:
https://www.facebook.com/AynRandOrg
Twitter: @AynRandOrg

Elks National Foundation
http://www.elks.org (click on Elks National
Foundation\Scholarships)
Facebook:
https://www.facebook.com/ElksNationalFoundation
Twitter: https://twitter.com/ElksNtnlFndtn

**The American Legion National High School
Oratorical Contest**
http://www.legion.org/oratorical
Facebook:
https://www.facebook.com/americanlegionhq
YouTube:
http://www.youtube.com/user/americanlegionHQ

SCHOLARSHIPS FOR THE DISABLED

National Center for Learning Disabilities: The Anne Ford and Allegra Ford Thomas Scholarship Award

http://www.ncld.org (click on About NCLD\Scholarships & Awards)
Facebook: https://www.facebook.com/NCLD.org
YouTube:
http://www.youtube.com/user/NCLD1401

National Federation of the Blind Scholarship Program

http://www.nfb.org (search for Scholarships)
Facebook: https://www.facebook.com/NationalFederationoftheBlind
Twitter: @NFB_voice
YouTube:
http://www.youtube.com/user/NationsBlind

Disability Care Center Scholarships

http://www.disabilitycarecenter.org (Search scholarships) or
https://www.disabilitycarecenter.org/giving-back/scholarships

Fred J. Epstein Youth Achievement Award

www.smartkidswithld.org
Facebook:
https://www.facebook.com/SmartKidsWithLD
Twitter: https://twitter.com/smartkidswld

MINORITY SCHOLARSHIPS

The Jackie Robinson Foundation
http://www.jackierobinson.org
Facebook: https://www.facebook.com/jrf42
Twitter: @JRFoundation

League of United Latin American Citizens (LULAC) National Scholarship Fund
http://www.lnesc.org
Facebook: https://www.facebook.com/LNESC
Twitter: @LNESC

Hispanic Scholarship Fund
http://www.hsf.net
Facebook:
https://www.facebook.com/HispanicScholarshipFund
Twitter: @HSFNews

Ron Brown Scholar Program
http://www.ronbrown.org
Facebook:
https://www.facebook.com/RonBrownScholarProgram
Twitter: @ronbrownscholar

GEM PhD Science Fellowship
http://www.gemfellowship.org
Facebook:
https://www.facebook.com/gem.consortium
Twitter: @GEMFellowship

Consortium for Graduate Study in Management
http://www.cgsm.org
Facebook: https://www.facebook.com/cgsm.org
Twitter: @cgsm_mba

The PhD Project
http://www.phdproject.com
Facebook:
https://www.facebook.com/thephdproject
Twitter: @ThePhDProject

Presbyterian Church—Native American Education Grant
http://www.presbyterianmission.org/ministries/finan
cialaid/native-american-education-grant
Facebook: https://www.facebook.com/pcusa
Twitter: @Presbyterian

INTERNATIONAL AND STUDY ABROAD SCHOLARSHIPS

The Rotary Foundation
http://www.rotary.org (click on Our
Programs\Scholarships)
Facebook: https://www.facebook.com/rotary
Twitter: @rotary
YouTube:
http://www.youtube.com/user/RotaryInternational

International Education Financial Aid
http://www.IEFA.org
Facebook:
https://www.facebook.com/internationalstudent
Twitter: @intstudent

EduPASS
http://www.edupass.org

EducationUSA
https://educationusa.state.gov
Facebook:
https://www.facebook.com/EducationUSA
Twitter: @educationusa

Institute of International Education (IIE)
Funding for U.S. Study
http://www.fundingusstudy.org
Facebook: https://www.facebook.com/IIEglobal
Twitter: @IIEglobal

Institute for the International Education of
Students (IES)
http://www.iesabroad.org
Facebook: https://www.facebook.com/IESAbroad
Twitter: @IESAbroad
YouTube: http://www.youtube.com/iesabroad

ScholarshipsCanada
http://www.scholarshipscanada.com
Facebook:
https://www.facebook.com/scholarshipscanada
Twitter: @ScholarshipsCA

Yconic (formerly Student Awards)
https://yconic.com
Facebook: https://www.facebook.com/yconic
Twitter: @yconicstudent

NONTRADITIONAL SCHOLARSHIPS

Soroptimist Live Your Dreams Awards
http://www.soroptimist.org
Facebook: https://www.facebook.com/Soroptimist-International-of-the-Americas-69575569890/
Twitter: @soroptimist

Executive Women International: Adult Students in Scholastic Transition (ASIST)
http://ewiconnect.com/
Facebook: https://www.facebook.com/ewicorp
Twitter: @EWICorporate

College Fish
http://www.collegefish.org
Facebook: https://www.facebook.com/collegefish
Twitter: @CollegeFish_4yr

To get more web addresses and information about various scholarship programs including new ones, visit http://www.scholarshipworkshop.com and join our newsletter group, or follow us on Facebook, http://www.facebook.com/scholarshipworkshop, or Twitter @ScholarshipWork.

2

Visiting General Web Sites

These sites may provide links to scholarship programs, give free scholarship and financial aid information, or administer scholarship programs. General web sites cover a broad range of information related to higher education and college funding:

- **The Scholarship Workshop**
  - o   www.scholarshipworkshop.com

- **The College Board**
  - o   www.collegeboard.org

- **FinAid**
  - o   www.finaid.org

- **The Princeton Review**
  - o   www.princetonreview.com (search scholarships)

- **Peterson's College Bound Home**
  - o   www.petersons.com

3

Using General Search Engines

Visit Yahoo!, Ask, Bing, and Google. Search for terms such as, "college scholarships," "financial aid," "scholarships," and "fellowships." Each of these search engines will give you a list of web sites and articles where the term you searched for is included. This will lead you to specific scholarship program web sites.

You can also use general search engines to find out if an organization you have heard about in the news or elsewhere has a web address. For example, if a news article lists a program called the Elks Most Valuable Student Scholarship, put the entire name into the search box of an engine with quotation marks around it. By doing this, you may be able to go directly to their web site if the search engine finds a link.

Also consider Google Alerts (see www.google.com/alerts) to get e-mail alerts for recent articles that have been written about scholarships, college, and financial aid. This is a wonderful way to get the latest information about current and new scholarships available.

4

Finding Magazine and News Articles About Scholarships on the Internet

Use a service such as Google Alerts or your public library web site to search for magazine and newspaper articles on the Internet about scholarships. With Google Alerts, you receive e-mails whenever the service finds results that include the information you want such as web pages, newspaper articles, or blog posts related to the search terms you entered for notification.

Alternatively, you could visit your local library on the Internet and use their online databases to search for magazine articles. Many of these articles list scholarship programs. Some magazines with previous articles are *Money*, *Ebony*, and *U.S. News & World Report*. You can also go directly to their web sites and perform a search on past articles. Often, many publications covering finance such as *Money* magazine publish articles about college aid. You can also conduct a search of articles relating to scholarships and financial aid by using *Google News* (https://news.google.com).

5

Discovering Scholarship Programs

Visit the web sites of organizations that administer or sponsor scholarships, awards, or fellowship programs. You should have a list of these after chapters 1 – 4. Many of these are included with social media references in chapter 1. For example, here are some organizations you can visit:

General Scholarships

Coca-Cola Scholars Foundation

- www.coca-colascholars.org

Veterans of Foreign Wars of the United States

- www.vfw.org (see Community – Youth and Education)

National YoungArts Foundation

- www.youngarts.org

The Ayn Rand Institute

- www.aynrand.org/contests

Elks National Foundation

- www.elks.org *(see Elks National Foundation - ENF Programs - Scholarships)*

The American Legion National High School Oratorical Contest

- www.legion.org/oratorical

Scholarship America Dream Award

- www.scholarshipamerica.org/dreamaward *(for current college students sophomore year and beyond)*

GE-Reagan Foundation Scholarship Program

- www.reaganfoundation.org/education/scholarship-programs

Military Commanders' Scholarship Fund

- http://sms.scholarsapply.org/militarycommanders

Central Intelligence Agency (CIA) Undergraduate Scholarship Program

- www.cia.gov *(see Careers & Internships, then Student Opportunities)*

Horatio Alger Scholarship Program

- https://scholars.horatioalger.org

Scholarships for the Disabled

National Center for Learning Disabilities - The Anne Ford and Allegra Ford Scholarship Award

- www.ncld.org *(see About NCLD - Scholarships & Awards)*

National Federation of the Blind Scholarship Program

- www.nfb.org

Wells Fargo Scholarship Program for People with Disabilities

- https://scholarsapply.org/pwdscholarship

RiSE Scholarship Foundation, Inc. Awards

- http://risescholarshipfoundation.org

Minority Scholarships

The Jackie Robinson Foundation

- www.jackierobinson.org

LULAC National Scholarship Fund

- www.lnesc.org

National Hispanic Scholarship Fund

- www.hsf.net

Ron Brown Scholar Program

- www.ronbrown.org

GEM PhD Science Fellowship

- www.gemfellowship.org

Consortium for Graduate Study in Management

- www.cgsm.org

The Ph. D. Project

- www.phdproject.org

International Scholarships

The Ayn Rand Institute - Anthem, The Fountainhead, and Atlas Shrugged Essay Contests

- www.aynrand.org/contests

The Rotary Foundation

- www.rotary.org

The Institute for the International Education of Students (IES)

- www.iesabroad.org

Nontraditional Scholarships

Soroptimist Live Your Dream Awards

- www.soroptimist.org

Cash Store Continuing Education Scholarship

- www.cashstore.com/scholarship *(for nontraditional students)*

6

Visiting Government Web Sites

Get information about federal and state aid available to you by visiting the following sites.

- **U. S. Department of Education**
    - www.ed.gov

- **Tax Benefits for Education**
    - www.irs.gov
    - (*see IRS Publication 970*)

Education Aid from States

Consult the education department, state grant agency or higher education agency in your area to get information about aid specific to students in your state. Review the list below and use a search engine to find the web page for the appropriate department or agency in your area.

Alabama
Alabama Commission on Higher Education
100 N. Union Street
P.O. Box 302000
Montgomery, AL 36130-2000
Phone: (334) 242-1998
Fax: (334) 242-0268
Website: http://www.ache.state.al.us

Alaska

Alaska Commission on Post-Secondary Education and
  Alaska Student Loan Corporation
P.O. Box 110505
Juneau, AK 99811-0505
Phone: (907) 465-2962, (800) 441-2962 (Alaska only)
Fax: (907) 465-5316
E-mail: ACPE@alaska.gov
Website: http://acpe.alaska.gov

Arizona

Arizona Commission for Post-Secondary Education
2020 North Central Avenue, Suite 650
Phoenix, AZ 85004-4503
Phone: (602) 258-2435
Fax: (602) 258-2483
Website: https://highered.az.gov/

Arkansas

Arkansas Department of Higher Education
Four Capitol Mall, Room 403-A
Little Rock, AR 72201
Phone: (501) 682-4475
Website: http://www.arkansased.org

California

California Student Aid Commission
P.O. Box 419026
Rancho Cordova, CA 95741-9026
Phone: 1 (888) CA GRANT (224-7268)
Fax: (916) 464-8002
E-mail: custsvcs@csac.ca.gov
Website: http://www.csac.ca.gov

Colorado
Colorado Department of Higher Education
201 East Colfax Avenue, Room 500
Denver, CO 80203
Phone: (303) 866-6600
Fax: (303) 830-0793
Website: http://www.cde.state.co.us/

Connecticut
CT Office of Higher Education
450 Columbus Boulevard, Suite 510
Hartford, CT 06103-1841
Phone: (860) 947-1800
Fax: (860) 947-1310
Website: http://www.ctohe.org

Delaware
DE Higher Education Office
The Townsend Building
401 Federal Street, Suite 2
Dover, DE 19901
Phone: (302) 735-4120, (800) 292-7935
Fax: (302) 739-5894
Website: https://www.doe.k12.de.us/ (*see Supports < Higher Ed*) or https://www.doe.k12.de.us/domain/226

District of Columbia
DC Office of the State Superintendent of Education
1050 1st Street, NE
Washington, DC 20002
Phone: (202) 727-6436
Website: https://osse.dc.gov/

Florida
Florida Department of Education

Office of Student Financial Assistance
325 West Gaines Street, Suite 1314
Tallahassee, Florida 32399–0400
Phone: (888) 827-2004
Website: http://www.floridastudentfinancialaid.org

Georgia
Georgia Student Finance Commission
State Loans and Grants Division
2082 East Exchange Place, Suite 200
Tucker, GA 30084
Phone: (800) 505-GSFC (4732
Fax: (770) 724-9089
Website: http://www.gsfc.org

Hawaii
Hawaii State Board of Education
P. O. Box 2360
Honolulu, HI 96804
Phone: (808) 586-3334
Fax: (808) 586-3433
Website: http://boe.hawaii.gov/
E-mail: BOE_Hawaii@notes.k12.hi.us

Idaho
Idaho State Board of Education
650 West State St.
P.O. Box 83720
Boise, ID 83720-0037
Phone: (208) 334-2270
Fax: (208) 334-2632
Website: http://www.boardofed.idaho.gov
E-mail: board@osbe.idaho.gov

Illinois
Illinois Student Assistance Commission
1755 Lake Cook Road
Deerfield, IL 60015-5209
Phone: (800) 899-4722

Fax: (847) 831-8549
Website: http://www.isac.org

Indiana
Indiana Commission for Higher Education
Division of Student Financial Aid
101 West Ohio Street, Suite 300
Indianapolis, IN 46204
Phone: (317) 464-4400 or Toll-Free: 1 (888) 528-4719
E-mail: awards@che.in.gov
Website: http://www.in.gov/ssaci

Iowa
Iowa College Student Aid Commission
430 E. Grand Avenue, 3rd Floor
Des Moines, IA 50309
Phone: (515) 725-3400 or (877) 272-4456
Fax: (515) 725-3401
Website: http://www.iowacollegeaid.gov

Kansas
Kansas Board of Regents
Student Financial Assistance
1000 SW Jackson St, Suite 520
Topeka, KS 66612-1368
Phone: (785) 430-4255 or (785) 430-4256
Fax: (785) 430-4233
Website: http://www.kansasregents.org

Kentucky
Kentucky Higher Education Assistance Authority
Student Aid Programs
P.O. Box 798
Frankfort, Kentucky 40602-0798
Phone: (800) 928-8926
Website: https://www.kheaa.com

Louisiana
LA Office of Student Financial Assistance

P.O. Box 91202
Baton Rouge, LA 70821-9202
Phone: (800) 259-5626
Fax: (225) 208-1496
Email: custserv@la.gov
Website: http://www.osfa.la.gov

Maine

Finance Authority of Maine
Maine Education Assistance Division
P. O. Box 949
5 Community Drive
Augusta, ME 04332-0949
Phone: (800) 228-3734
Fax: (207) 623-0095
E-mail: education@famemaine.com
Website: http://www.famemaine.com

Maryland

Maryland Higher Education Commission
6 North Liberty Street, Ground Suite
Baltimore, Maryland 21201
Phone: (410) 767-3300 or Toll-Free: 1 (800) 974-0203
Fax: (410) 332-0250
Email: osfamail.mhec@maryland.gov
Website: http://www.mhec.state.md.us

Massachusetts

The Massachusetts Office of Student Financial Assistance
75 Pleasant Street
Malden, Massachusetts 02148
Phone: (617) 391-6070
Fax: (617) 391-6085
Email: osfa@osfa.mass.edu
Website: http://www.mass.edu/osfa/

Michigan

MI Student Aid
Student Scholarships and Grants

P.O. Box 30462
Lansing, MI 48909-7962
Phone: 1 (888) 447-2687
Website: http://www.michigan.gov/mistudentaid
Email: mistudentaid@michigan.gov

Minnesota
Minnesota Office of Higher Education
1450 Energy Park Drive, Suite 350
Saint Paul, MN 55108-5227
Phone: (651) 642-0567 or Toll-Free: 1 (800) 657-3866
Fax: (651) 642-0675
Website: http://www.ohe.state.mn.us

Mississippi
Board of Trustees
Mississippi Institutions of Higher Learning
3825 Ridgewood Road
Jackson, MS 39211-6453
Phone: (601) 432-6997, in state only: (800) 327-2980
E-mail: sfa@ihl.state.ms.us
Website: http://www.mississippi.edu

Missouri
MO Department of Higher Education
205 Jefferson Street
P.O. Box 1469
Jefferson City, MO 65102-1469
Phone: (573) 751-2361 or Toll-Free: (800) 473-6757
Fax: (573) 751-6635
E-mail: info@dhe.mo.gov
Website: https://dhe.mo.gov/

Montana
Montana Office of the Commissioner of Higher
  Education
560 N. Park, 4th Floor
P.O. Box 203201
Helena, MT 59620-9124

Phone: (406) 449-6570
Fax: (406) 449-9171
Website: http://www.mus.edu/che

Nebraska
NE Coordinating Commission for
 Postsecondary Education
140 N. Eighth Street, Suite 300
P.O. Box 95005
Lincoln. NE 68509-5005
Phone: (402) 471-2847
Website: https://ccpe.nebraska.gov/

Nevada
Nevada Department of Education, Financial Aid
700 East 5th Street
Carson City, NV 89701
Phone: (775) 687-9200
Fax: (775) 687-9101
Website: http://www.doe.nv.gov

New Hampshire
New Hampshire Department of Education
101 Pleasant Street
Concord. NH 03301-3494
Phone: (603) 271-3494
Fax: (603) 271-1953
Website: https://www.education.nh.gov/

New Jersey
New Jersey Higher Education Student Assistance
Authority
P. O. Box 540
Trenton, NJ 08625
Phone: (609) 584-4480, (800) 792-8670
Website: http://www.hesaa.org

New Mexico
New Mexico Higher Education Department

2044 Galisteo Street, Suite 4
Santa Fe, NM 87505-2100
Phone: (505) 476-8400
Website: http://hed.state.nm.us

New York
New York State Higher Education Services Corporation
99 Washington Avenue
Albany, NY 12255
Phone: (518) 473-1574, (888) 697-4372
Website: http://www.hesc.ny.gov

North Carolina
NC State Education Assistance Authority
P.O. Box 14103
Research Triangle Park, NC 27709
Phone: (919) 549-8614
Fax: (919) 549-8481
E-mail: information@ncseaa.edu
Website: http://www.ncseaa.edu
> College Foundation of North Carolina
> P.O. Box 41966
> Raleigh, NC 27629-1966
> Phone: (866) 866-2362
> Website: https://www.cfnc.org

North Dakota
ND University System
10th Floor, State Capitol
600 East Boulevard Avenue, Dept 215
Bismarck, ND 58505-0230
Phone: (701) 328-2960
Fax: (701) 328-2961
E-mail: ndus.office@ndus.edu
Website: http://www.ndus.edu

Ohio
Ohio Department of Education
25 South Front Street

Columbus, OH 43215
Phone: (614) 466-6000
Fax: (614) 466-5866
E-mail: hotline@highered.ohio.gov
Website: https://www.ohiohighered.org

Oklahoma

Oklahoma State Regents for Higher Education
655 Research Parkway, Suite 200
Oklahoma City, OK 73104
Phone: (405) 225-9100
E-mail: communicationsdepartment@osrhe.edu
Website: http://www.okhighered.org

Oregon

Oregon Higher Education Coordinating Commission
Office of Student Access & Completion
1500 Valley River Drive, Suite 100
Eugene, OR 97401
Phone: (541) 687-7400
Fax: (541) 687-7414
Website: http://oregonstudentaid.gov

Pennsylvania

Pennsylvania Higher Education Assistance
  Agency (PHEAA)
P.O. Box 8157
Harrisburg, PA 17105-8157
Phone: (800) 692-7392
Fax: (717) 720-3786
Website: http://www.pheaa.org

Rhode Island

Rhode Island Office of the Postsecondary Commissioner
560 Jefferson Boulevard, Suite 100
Warwick, RI 02886
Phone: (401) 736-1100
Fax: (401) 732-3541
Website: https://www.riopc.edu/

South Carolina
SC Higher Education Tuition Grants Commission
115 Atrium Way, Suite 102
Columbia, SC 29223
Phone: (803) 896-1120
E-mail: info@sctuitiongrants.org
Website: http://www.sctuitiongrants.com

South Dakota
South Dakota Board of Regents
306 East Capitol Ave
Suite 200
Pierre, SD 57501-2545
Phone: (605) 773-3455
Fax: (605) 773-5320
E-mail: info@sdbor.edu
Website: http://www.sdbor.edu

Tennessee
TN Higher Education Commission
404 James Robertson Parkway, Suite 1900
Nashville, TN 37243-0820
Phone: (615) 741-3605
Website: https://www.tn.gov/thec

Texas
TX Higher Education Coordinating Board
P.O. Box 12788
Austin, TX 78711-2788
Phone: (512) 427-6101
Website: http://www.thecb.state.tx.us

Utah
Utah Higher Education Assistance Authority
60 South 400 West
Salt Lake City, UT 84101
Phone: (801) 321-7294, (877) 336-7378
Fax: (801) 366-8431
Website: http://www.uheaa.org

Vermont
VT Student Assistance Corporation
Champlain Mill
P.O. Box 2000
Winooski, VT 05404-2601
Phone: (802) 655-4050
Fax: (802) 654-3765
E-mail: info@vsac.org
Website: http://www.vsac.org

Virginia
State Council of Higher Education for Virginia
James Monroe Building, Tenth Floor
101 N. Fourteenth Street
Richmond, VA 23219
Phone: (804) 225-2600
Fax: (804) 225-2604
Website: http://www.schev.edu

Washington
WA Student Achievement Council
P. O. Box 43430
917 Lakeridge Way, SW
Olympia, WA 98504-3430
Phone: (360) 753-7800
E-mail: info@wsac.wa.gov
Website: http://www.wsac.wa.gov

West Virginia
West Virginia Higher Education Policy Commission
1018 Kanawha Boulevard East, Suite 700
Charleston, WV 25301
Phone: (304) 558-2101
Fax: (304) 558-1011
Website: http://www.wvhepc.edu/

Wisconsin
Higher Educational Aids Board
Post Office Box 7885

Madison, WI 53707-7885
Phone: (608) 267-2206
Fax: (608) 267-2808
E-mail: HEABmail@wi.gov
Website: http://www.heab.state.wi.us

Wyoming
Wyoming State Department of Education
122 W. 25th Street, Suite E200
Cheyenne, WY 82002
Phone: (307) 777-7675
Fax: 307-777-6234
Website: https://edu.wyoming.gov/

7

Connecting to College and University Web pages

Use information in this chapter to get information about scholarship dollars at various schools including those who are at the top of your list. You can find most colleges on the Internet by typing their name or abbreviated name into your browser and adding (.edu). For example, the Florida A & M University (FAMU) web site address is www.famu.edu. The George Washington University web site address is www.gwu.edu. Or you could visit a search engine and type in the name of the school and find their web site address.

For a general listing of colleges and universities, visit https://www.petersons.com. Also visit www.collegeboard.com to research a specific school and its financial aid. With the College Board website, you can get information about the percentage of financial need met by specific colleges and universities within their database. This website may also offer scholarships you can become eligible for by completing steps in your college journey such as building your list of potential colleges and universities, practicing for the SAT, improving your SAT score, and completing the FAFSA.

8

Looking Closer to Home

Visit your high school counselor or career center to see if their office maintains or plans to maintain a web page for the school with information about available local and state scholarships. In addition to high schools, some county school systems maintain databases of scholarships that are available to students in the county.

Investigate the web sites of local radio and television stations, newspapers, companies, banks, and social organizations to see if they offer aid to students in your community. And don't forget to visit your church or faith based organization's web site if it has one.

Have you ever entered a search term in the main search box and received millions of results or advertising pop-ups that really aren't relevant? An advanced search will help you cut through the clutter. You can use the advanced search function in a general search engine such as Google or Yahoo! to find specific information for your scholarship search especially for local and regional opportunities. An advanced search helps narrow the results you might get from an Internet search. You can use the advanced search in a general search engine to find community foundations in your city. Scholarships administered or offered by community foundations in your area will primarily be open to local students. In a search engine such as Google or Yahoo!, type advanced search into the main search area. The results you get should include links to the advanced search areas of their site. The advanced search page should appear similar to the image below.

Advanced Search		
Find Results	all of these words	Arlington
	the exact phrase	community foundation
	with at least one of these words	Virginia
	any of these words	

The image above shows an advanced search performed to find a community foundation in the city of Arlington, Virginia. This search uncovered the Arlington Community Foundation. Many com-munity foundations such as the Arlington Com-munity Foundation maintain a list along with applications for scholarships available to students in specific counties or service areas. The Berks County Community Foundation in Pennsylvania does this also. There are community foundations throughout the United States. There may be one in your community too! So make sure to conduct an advanced search to find one available to you in your area.

Conduct this type of search if you are looking for specific types of scholarships as well. For example, you may be interested in scholarships for culinary school. With an advanced search you might enter the exact phrase as "culinary arts," at least one of the words as "scholarships," and for all of the words, "associations." This will help you find associations that offer or administer scholarships in the field of culinary arts.

9

Getting Required Forms and Testing Information

You can complete the FAFSA and register or practice for standardized tests on the Internet also. Taking the SAT or ACT and completing the FAFSA are required steps to apply for many scholarships.

- **Free Application for Federal Student Aid (FAFSA)**
    - o www.fafsa.ed.gov

- **FAFSA4caster**
    (estimate your eligibility for federal student aid)
    - o www.fafsa4caster.ed.gov

- **College Board**
    - o www.collegeboard.org

- **SAT Preparation Center**
    - o https://collegereadiness.collegeboard.org /sat/practice

- **ACT Online**
    - o www.actstudent.org

10

Avoiding Scams

Be Warned! Even though you see information on the Internet that looks legitimate, it may not be, especially if it sounds too good to be true. Visit the Federal Trade Commission's web site to check fraud alerts.

- **Federal Trade Commission**
  - www.ftc.gov

Also check with your counselor, career center director, or an educational advisor or counselor to get their advice. They may have seen offers you should definitely avoid.

11

An Important Reminder

Using the Internet alone without other resources such as books, newspapers, magazines, personal telephone calls, and research in your community will not make your scholarship search complete. Much information on the Internet is national in scope and will not capture opportunities that may be in your very own backyard. Devoting time and effort to your search in several ways as explained in the next chapter could pay off greatly in the future!

12

Beyond the Internet Search

For a comprehensive search that gives you the best and most opportunities to win scholarship money, devote close attention to these areas as well as the Internet!

Library Search

To start your scholarship journey, you should go to the nearest library. Once there, do the following:

- Look for scholarship directories such as the *Ultimate Scholarship Book* or *Scholarships, Grants & Prizes* from Peterson's.
- Search for books such as *Winning Scholar-ships for College* that go beyond the standard listing found in a scholarship directory. The focus for books of this type is to help you learn how to win scholarships. As a result, they may have limited listings but each listing would include as much additional information on winning the scholarship as possible.
- Search for newspaper articles about scholarships. Newspapers such as *USA Today* periodically have articles about getting money for college. To find articles in sources like these as well as the magazines above, use the library's online database or microfiche. In addition, an Internet resource you can use would be Google

Alerts explained earlier in this resource.

Local Search

The local search is one most often ignored by the typical student. Usually someone searching for scholarships uses a few scholarship directories and an Internet search service such as www.fastweb.com. For some students in search of college money, an Internet search service is the only resource used. Although search services similar to www.fastweb.com can be wonderful, you should not ignore other sources to find funding. If your scholarship quest includes directories and the Internet only or even just the Internet, you could be overlooking some valuable scholarship opportunities.

The best way to have a complete scholarship search is to search locally in your community, state, and region as well as using directories and the Internet. Most of the scholarships you find in directories and on the Internet are national which means that if you apply, you are among many others who hope to win the scholarship. This makes winning the scholarship harder because it is more competitive. For many local scholarships, the number of applications received from students is much smaller which makes them less competitive. This is probably because local scholarships are generally smaller in monetary value and a lot of students feel they aren't worth the time and effort. Fortunately smaller, easier to win scholarships, do add up and should definitely not be ignored. In my scholarship total of more than $400,000, awards as small as $50.00 were included. And my daughter won a small local scholarship when she was eight years old for the area where we live.

For a local scholarship search, you should do the following.

- Search for community foundations. Visit www.cfnova.org for an example of a community foundation and the scholarships they might offer. Visit chapter 8 to learn how to conduct an advanced Internet search for community foundations and local scholarship information.

- Research local clubs and organizations. Examples of these would be the Soroptimist Club, the Optimist Club, Exchange Clubs of America, Daughters of the American Revolution, YMCA/YWCA, the Kiwanis Club, the Rotary Club, the Lions Club, or the Knights of Columbus. Also look for sororities and fraternities. For more examples of clubs and organizations based in local communities throughout the United States, read Chapter 2 of *Winning Scholarships for College* (fifth edition). Optimist International, an organization that has local clubs throughout the country, has an oratorical and an essay contest for students under age 19 where they can win up to $2500 in scholarships. I competed in the oratorical contest for the local Optimist Club in my area over 25 years ago and won quite a few awards in the process. Although I did not win the scholarship, the experience helped to develop many of the communication and writing skills that I have used successfully throughout my life.

- Contact companies and banks located in your community. Some may have scholarships available to local residents. Call the personnel or human resource department of these companies to inquire if they offer scholarships to students in the community.

- Ask your parents to check with their employers. Some employers offer scholarships to children of their employees.

- If your parents belong to a work-related union, contact the union to find out if they offer scholarships to the children of their members. Union Plus is an example of a non-profit organization that maintains a scholarship program for union members.

- Contact any organization to which you or your parents belong, local or national, to determine whether they have a scholarship program for their members. Your church or faith related organization might be an example.

- Since some credit unions have scholarship opportunities for their members, you should also contact your credit union, if you have one.

13

Crowdfunding and Social Media

Crowdfunding allows students to tell their story over the Internet to thousands of people quickly and with minimal effort. Individuals all over the world with access to the Internet see a student's words and hopefully become compelled to contribute with funding. There are several popular crowdfunding sites such as www.gofundme.com or www.gogetfunding. com.

Following are some tips for a successful crowdfunding campaign:

- You should have great visuals. If you can take a picture of yourself with something from your future college or university, like a sign or mascot, it might help to encourage alumni and others to donate because it may give them an immediate visual connection with you.

- Use social media. Let others know about your campaign on your social media accounts but ask ALL of your family members with active social media accounts to share. If you attend a church or faith based organization, ask them to share on their social media. Also contact the youth and young adult ministry, scholarship ministry, education ministry and similar ministries to let them know about your campaign.

- Don't forget to create a hashtag specific to your campaign. This can make it easier to follow your campaign and see the interest it's getting.
- Check with your current or future university to see how you can connect with alumni via social media, email, or another way to share your campaign. Also check out the web site and social media accounts for the alumni association in your hometown.
- Give a compelling and interesting name to your campaign. It should be something that people can easily remember. For example, *Amy Needs Your Dollars for College - I Could Be Your Future Physician.*
- Post updates. Let people know how it's going for you. Share success and failure. And let them know how much you appreciate the money already contributed and how wonderful it will be when you reach your campaign goal. You might also share what you've done with money contributed so far.
- Offer an incentive. You could offer something like a free hour of live or web based tutoring for one student at the local high school or middle school for every $100 or $1000 you receive. Or you could offer to spread the love by helping at a food bank, a shelter or some other community organization one hour per month every time you reach a $1000 threshold (or some other number) in your campaign.
- In your story, share your future career plans and how you plan to help others in the future just like donors will hopefully help you now. For example, you could discuss setting up a mentoring program or joining an organization such as Big Brothers

Big Sisters once you graduate. Or for those with family members affiliated with a Greek organization mention future participation in the community service efforts of those organizations (if you success-fully pledge).

- Let donors know exactly how the money will be used. For example: I need $5,000 for my room and board deposit at XYZ university.
- Consider adding a video to your story. Something memorable would be best. People love videos with animals. Maybe include your favorite pet in a video saying how much you will miss him or her doing their favorite stunt while you're away at college. But you're planning for a great future for both of you in your own home after you graduate. Or perhaps the video could be of you showcasing a special skill or talent you plan to share with others as a future college student or graduate.

Crowdfunding is a great way to raise last minute cash for school. However, your funding campaign may not raise as much as you want or need. You should make every effort to explore additional sources of funding explained in other sections of this guide. Also don't forget to explore scholarships, grants and awards for current college students. Don't stop looking for additional funding until all your current and future college bills are fully funded.

14

Online Applications

For colleges and universities, getting an application is relatively easy. For private organizations and companies, getting an application may require a little more work. However, for some large scholarship pro-grams administered or offered by private companies and organizations, downloading applications from web sites and applying online is very popular. Many students prefer applying online because it's quicker and easier. Unfortunately, it's also very easy to make mistakes and to give answers, especially short essay answers, that don't reflect a lot of thought.

With your online applications, follow these guidelines:

- Print online applications first without completing them
- Complete them on paper
- Then transfer your answers from paper to your computer in the online application
- Print the completed application
- Proofread
- If you like everything and have no mistakes, press SEND or whatever button you need to press online to send the application. If you can, make a PDF copy of the applications you complete. This can make it easier to review your application to get ready for a potential

interview.

An impressive application can help you stand out well amongst others.

15

Winning Elements

What are winning elements? Winning elements are items that set you apart from the crowd. And although you may be using the Internet primarily for your applications, try to include winning elements as much as possible. Remember! Completing applications is important but understanding strategies you can use to help you win are even more important. Read on for more about winning elements for your scholarship quest:

Your résumé/activity list

Your extracurricular activities, leadership positions, community involvement, and your being a well-rounded student are very important to winning scholarships. To show your involvement in an organized manner with a résumé or an activity list closely resembling a professional résumé helps scholarship programs and educational institutions see your participation and leadership as a whole unit rather than scattered among a few lines on an application.

Essays

Essays are also very important to your winning a scholarship. An essay gives you an opportunity to really shine and tell those who read it how you feel about a particular issue or the essay can showcase how well you can interpret a contest theme. An essay can help you to elaborate on activities you've outlined in your résumé/activity list. In fact, incorporating your activities, how they have helped to make you into the student or person you are, and how these activities may have helped others, are important features to include in an essay and make its content come alive for the readers, while showing your best qualities.

Samples of your work

If you have done anything extraordinary or award-winning or that has received some type of recognition, include a sample as part of your appl-ication package. For example, in my scholarship search, I included an award winning layout from the high school literary magazine where I was the editor. I also included poetry that had won awards as well. In one of my applications, I even included a poem I had written titled, "I Am a Child." I liked the poem and thought it represented my writing style and how I felt about life. It also coincided with my essay where I had written about using my journalism skills (gained through my extracurricular activities) to overcome poverty and destruction in America. The poem which had this line, "I am a child yet I have seen cruelty in the face of kind-ness," fit the theme of my application essay. For the essay, I had to answer the question, "You are at your 30th high school reunion. The president of the United States is part of your class. Yet, you are the guest of honor. Why?"

Make sure you don't go overboard when including samples of your work as part of your application package. One or two items you feel are appropriate are enough. Don't send anything that won't fit in a 9" X 11" envelope. And most importantly, if you are asked NOT to send anything extra, DON'T.

By the way, if you write poetry, you may be able to win a scholarship or award in the Scholastic Art & Writing Awards and get recognized in the National Student Poet program. This program is open to students in grades 9 through 11.

Articles

These articles could be on you or your activities (even if the article doesn't mention your name specifically). If you have been a part of an activity or if you started an activity that has been written about in your local newspaper or college newspaper, include a copy of the article. Once again, don't go overboard. One article, if you're also sending samples of your work is enough. Two articles should be your maximum if you're not including samples of your work.

Recommendations
(more details in the next section)

Some programs will ask for recommendations. If they do, great! If they don't, you can still include one if it's really good. A wonderful recommendation can help your cause even if it isn't requested by a scholarship program. An outstanding recommendation from a well-regarded individual, just like other winning elements can help to overcome a less than stellar GPA and for some programs, winning could be based entirely on a recommendation or nomination.

Résumé/Activity List

One of the best ways students can set themselves apart from others is through their extracurricular activities, especially with those that are community based. Many organizations are very impressed by students who are involved in the community and in their college or university. To show your involvement in an organized and impressive way, you can include a résumé or activity list with your applications. Although most applications will ask you about your activities and include lines for you to list them, your activities look better when presented as a whole and in a résumé-like format. Some students are using the word processing wonders available today to make beautiful résumés complete with pictures and graphic elements that anyone would be proud to show in a job interview. That's the idea. It's great if you have a scholarship judge looking at your résumé/activity list and not only being impressed by what you've done but also how you presented it. Just make sure you don't overdo it with pictures and graphic elements. Content is the most important factor.

For example, you could organize your résumé in the following manner.

Departmental Clubs/Activities
Here list all activities you are involved in within your school

Student Council – 2017 to present
List activity and years in which you participated

National Beta Club – 2018
List any positions of leadership held and year held as a subheading

Future Business Leaders of America – 2018 to present

Honorary Clubs
* List all organizations that you have been inducted into because of outstanding performance *

National Honors Society - 2018

Community Clubs/Service Activities
List clubs or activities within the community

Role Models and Leaders Program – 2016 to present

Macon City Volunteer Youth Coach – 2017 to present

NAACP – 2018 to present

Susan G. Komen Race for the Cure – 2017 to present

Community Church Youth Group – 2016 to present

Work/Internship/Research Experience

Laura's Babysitting Services – 2016 to present

Awards/Honors
List all the awards that you have won.

Volleyball Team's Most Valuable Newcomer – 2017

Certificate of Participation – Core Advisory Day – 2017

President's Student Service Award – 2018

You can find other types of résumés in the fifth edition of *Winning Scholarships for College*. Different formats are acceptable as long as your résumé is easily readable and well-presented.

Recommendations

Another area where students can stand out from the crowd is through the recommendations of others. In order to get the best recommendations you need to be careful about who you ask, how you ask, and when you ask. Here are a few tools to help you do that.

First consider the scholarship you are applying for. Even if the program is not requesting a recommendation, include one anyway especially if the recommendation is a good one or it highlights your community involvement. Nearly all scholar-ship programs are impressed by those with com-munity involvement. If the program is re-questing a recommendation, try to get at least one from an individual that fits the nature of the scholarship. For example, if it's for a STEM (Science, Technology, Engineering and Math) type of scholarship, get your physics, chemistry or another teacher in a related field to write one.

In general, you should get recommendations from the following if you can:

- a teacher or professor
- a counselor or administrator
- a coordinator for a community based activity

- your minister or another clergyman if you have one
- anyone other than a relative who can discuss your most impressive qualities in a written format.

As you think of people to include on your recommendation resource list, make sure to include a sentence about they how they know of you. This will help you to pick and choose individuals to write recommendations as you begin applying for multiple scholarships. Also when pondering who you should ask, think about whether the person is accustomed to writing recommendations for stu-dents or if they might be a good writer. If they have never written a recommendation and/or they aren't a good writer, your recommendation could be a nightmare or a "one liner."

When you ask for a recommendation, do the following:

- Give a written description of the scholarship and/or program
- Include your résumé and any extras you plan to send with your scholarship application
- Include a self-addressed stamped envelope with two stamps (if the recommendation needs to be sent in the U.S. mail)
- Ask at least four weeks before deadline
- Follow-up to see how they are doing or if they need additional information
- Send thank you notes or e-mails. You may need to ask again.
- *Winning Scholarships for College* (fifth edition)

includes a sample letter requesting a recommendation as well as an example recommendation chart to help you keep track of recommendations and their due dates.

16

The Essay

Although there are many types of scholarships you can find via the Internet and social media in varying amounts, the largest scholarships generally require you to write an essay or to explain your ideas in writing. For most essays you can use the following five paragraph format particularly if writing is difficult for you. If writing is one of your strengths, there is no need to follow the five paragraph format. Just make sure your essay is interesting and includes details about your extracurricular activities and/or your life.

I. INTRODUCTION - ONE PARAGRAPH

- Use a quotation, poem, thought, amazing fact, idea, question, or simple statement to draw your reader into your topic.
- The main idea does not have to be stated in the first sentence, but it should definitely lead to and be related to your main idea or thesis statement, which should introduce three main points you will develop in the body of your essay.
- Avoid using statements such as, "I am going to talk about . . . " or "This essay is about . . ."

II. BODY - THREE PARAGRAPHS

- Support the main idea with facts, thoughts, ideas, published poetry, quotes, and other intriguing, insightful material that will captivate your audience.
- Present clear images.
- If necessary, use a thesaurus to ensure you are not using the same words repeatedly. Using a word over and over will become monotonous for your audience and distract them from your subject.

III. CONCLUSION - ONE PARAGRAPH

- Restate the main idea in an original way.
- You can again use a poem or quotation to leave an impression. However, avoid using this tactic in all three parts of the essay. It may appear repetitious and unoriginal.
- Refer to the future in terms of your plans pertaining to the subject of your essay. For example, in an essay describing your future career goals, refer to yourself in the career that you have outlined. This reference should project you, and the ideas you presented in the essay, into the future.

* Special Note - Using quotations or poems can show that you are well read. If your essay looks like a dumping ground for quotes and the words of another, using quotations and poems could show something else entirely. Be selective and look for quotes that are enlightening and profound.

As you become more experienced with writing essays you can expand on the format by including more paragraphs or even reducing the number of paragraphs and abandoning the format. If you start with the basic five paragraph format, it is easy to adapt and change to fit the style of your essay, as I did when I wrote an essay for the Coca-Cola scholarship which had nine paragraphs. I also changed the format to write an essay that had only two paragraphs. You can read both essays and an analysis of each in Chapter 11 of *Winning Scholarships for College*.

Early in your scholarship search prepare two basic essays following the format above. The essays can easily be tailored later to fit most scholarship application essay requirements.

Since many essays require descriptions of you and your future career goals, let's follow the format to write an essay about you; featuring your activities. In nearly all of the essays I wrote to win scholarships, I incorporated information about specific activities in which I was involved. Once you finish, this essay and parts of it (recycling) can probably be used for every essay you write regardless of the question.

If you have an essay you need to write for a scholarship immediately, it will help if you do the following activities first.

- Finish your résumé/activity list if you haven't already. This needs to be done before you begin any essay. Using the information from your résumé/activity list, you should include additional details about your activities to support the main points of your essay. Scholarship organizations are very impressed by students who are involved in various endeavors beyond typical classroom work. Showing your passion and commitment to certain activities by including more information about your involvement will help you stand out from the crowd of other applicants. Refer to the chapter, "Grades Don't Mean Everything," in *Winning Scholarships for College* for more information and also the Winning Elements section in this publication.

- Research the organization or company sponsoring the scholarship or award.
- Learn why the scholarship was established and the mission of the organization. If one or more of your activities fit the reasoning behind why the scholarship was established or the organization's mission you may want to highlight this in your essay.
- Understand the question. Think of several ways you might answer and write them down.
- Look at the scholarship application. What do most of the questions focus on: academics, community involvement, etc.? If an organization asks most of its application questions about community involvement, then try to build your essay around activities you do that benefit the community.

Since you are writing a descriptive essay about you or your future career goals, featuring your activities, the next step is to think of three adjectives that describe you. For each adjective, write down an activity that fits with that adjective. For example, the five paragraph essay format would now look like the following:

I. INTRODUCTION - ONE PARAGRAPH

   A. Adjective/Noun 1
   B. Adjective/Noun 2
   C. Adjective/Noun 3

II. BODY - THREE PARAGRAPHS

  A. Adjective/Noun 1

     1. Activity 1
     2. Activity 2
     3. Activity 3

  B. Adjective/Noun 2

     1. Activity 1
     2. Activity 2
     3. Activity 3

  C. Adjective/Noun 3

     1. Activity 1
     2. Activity 2
     3. Activity 3

Note: You do not need three activities for each. If you have only two, that's okay.

III. CONCLUSION - ONE PARAGRAPH

    A. Summarize your adjectives and how they relate to you and your activities. Refer to the future.

As you write about activities in your essay, don't just list them as you did with your résumé/activity list. If you do, the essay is really saying nothing more than you already did. When you write about your activities, you should be answering these questions as part of your essay:

1. What is the activity?
2. Who does the activity benefit?
3. When do you participate in this activity?
4. Where do you participate in this activity?
5. How does this activity benefit you or others?
6. Why are you involved in the activity?

Based on the outline, adjectives, activities, and answers to the above questions, you could begin your essay like the example below, assuming the adjectives you chose were self-motivated, energetic, and compassionate:

When I think of the words self-motivated, energetic, and compassionate, I think of myself. For the past seven years, starting in elementary, into middle school and now my first two years in high school, I have part-

icipated in many activities that reflect these words. More than just words, they really describe who I am and how I feel about life.

For example, in terms of self-motivation, I built a web site and social media page for students interested in getting tutors at our middle school and continued maintaining it during high school. Building the web site and populating it with insightful content was a frustrating and challenging task I set for myself. It took me most of the summer before my freshman year at XYZ High School, but I finished it to the amazement of my parents and friends. The web site, once completed, became a much-needed reference for students in our community to find tutors and other information to help them in all types of subjects. The web site also helped the upper-class students who became tutors make a little money to get a jump-start on college expenses. Most importantly, for those who weren't interested in charging, the site helped those who just wanted to aid their peers and apply principles they learned in class.

As a freshman at XYZ High School, I began to show more of my energetic traits by participating in several athletic activities concurrently which really challenged my self-motivation and determination, but most importantly helped me to relearn the value of teamwork and cooperation for all en-

deavors. I joined the volleyball team. I became a university cheerleader . . .

The next paragraph would focus on compassionate. The last paragraph would be a summary and conclusion. This essay is an example of a rough draft for a descriptive essay using the adjectives self-motivated, energetic, and compassionate. It still needs work but it's meant to give you an idea of how to structure your essay using the adjectives or nouns you selected and the examples of your activities that could fit the adjectives or nouns you selected.

To get additional information about planning your essays, choosing adjectives, writing about your activities, and writing different types of essays, read *The Scholarship & College Essay Planning Kit.*

17

Application Checklist

Use the following checklist to make sure you've done all you need to do as you receive new applications and send out completed ones.

1.   All applications should be typed, no exceptions — unless the application requests that you print. If so, use black ink.

2.   Make photocopies of applications as you receive them or download them as PDF's to a folder on your computer. To avoid mistakes in the future, complete the applications well ahead of the deadline. Also make a list of frequently asked questions and their answers. Always keep a copy of your completed applications. You may need them to prepare for interviews.

3.   Set up a file system for all copies of applications so you can locate them easily as deadlines draw near. A file system is also helpful because you can refer to an application for information to use on another one. Electronic file folders using Windows Explorer are great as well.

4.   All sections of the application that you are not directly responsible for should be given to those who are responsible for them as soon as possible. Recommend-

ation forms for counselors, advisors and administrators are some examples. This is especially important when completing online applications. It is very easy to forget the sections others need to complete for you.

5. If you apply for a scholarship online, print the application first. Complete it. Then complete the application online. Print it again and proofread before you hit the SEND button. It is very easy to make mistakes on electronic applications.

6. Include your personal résumé/activity list. Most applications have space for you to list your activities and special awards, but it looks more professional to include a résumé. Never leave the spaces for this information blank. Instead, type instructions to see additional information on a separate sheet. The separate sheet will be your résumé.

7. Type essays and other supporting material on good quality paper. Use paper with a weight of at least 24 lb.

8. With your application include articles that may have appeared in your local newspaper about you or your activities.

9. Include samples of your work that are extraordinary, or award-winning. Don't be afraid to send along copies of poetry, artwork, or audio recordings of your special talents, which may include sing-ing or dancing or playing the piano. If you have any special talent or hobby, flaunt it.

It makes your application stand out from others. When you include extra information, make sure it really is out-standing or extraordinary. And don't over-load your application with extra material. Include no more than one or two examples of outstanding work. If possible, try to make sure that all of your material will fit into a 9" X 12" envelope. Most importantly, if a scholarship program or college/university re-quests that you not include additional information, don't. And please be aware, sending additional paper based information is usually better than sending something such as a CD. Scholarship committees usually don't have an opportunity to stop reading applications to pop in a musical compilation unless music is the basis of the competition.

10. Some programs that issue applications specifically request that additional pages or supporting information and examples be kept to a minimum if they are allowed at all. Respect their wishes.

11. For questions that do not apply to you, write "not applicable" in the answer blank, or abbreviated "NA," to show that you have not overlooked the question.

12. Make a recommendations list. You may be required to list the names and e-mail addresses of your references on your application. Some scholarship programs ask for this so that they can send recommendation forms to these individuals

directly, without using the student as a medium.

Other Resources from Marianne Ragins

Books and Publications

The Scholarship & College Essay Planning Kit
- If you have trouble getting beyond a blank page when it comes to writing an essay, this resource is for you.

Get Money for College – An Audio Series
- If you don't have time to read a book or attend a class but you do have time to listen, this audio series can help you learn how to find and win scholarships for college.

10 Steps for Using the Internet in Your Scholarship Search
- This is a resource designed to be used at your computer to walk you step by step through using the Internet for your scholarship search. It keeps you from being overwhelmed by the massive amount of sometimes misleading information found on the web. This resource is updated yearly.

The Scholarship Monthly Planning Calendar
- This convenient and easy to use monthly planning calendar will help you with time management, getting organized, and staying on track with activities to meet major scholarship and award deadlines. This resource is updated yearly.

Winning Scholarships for College
- In *Winning Scholarships for College*, Marianne Ragins, the winner of more than $400,000 in scholarship funds, proves that it`s not always the students with the best grades or the highest SAT scores

who win scholarships. Whether you are in high school, returning to or currently enrolled in college, or planning to study abroad, this easy to follow college scholarship guide will show you the path to scholarship success. One of the most comprehensive books on winning scholarships and written by a successful scholarship recipient, it reveals where and how to search for funds, and walks you step by step through the scholar-ship application process.

Last Minute College Financing Guide
- If you have an acceptance letter, but you are wondering how to pay the tuition bill because you just started searching for college money, this resource is for you!

Workshops & Boot Camps

The Scholarship Workshop Presentation
- In The Scholarship Workshop presentation which is a 1, 2, or 3 hour interactive seminar, speaker Marianne Ragins proves that it is not always the student with the best grades or the highest SAT scores who wins scholarships. Instead she shows students of all ages that most scholarships are awarded to students who exhibit the best preparation. By attending The Scholar-ship Workshop presentation, a student will be well prepared to meet the challenge of finding and winning scholarships. The presentation is designed to help students conduct a successful scholarship search from the research involved in finding scholarship money to the scholarship essays, scholarship interview tips and strategies involved in winning them. This presentation is usually sponsored by various organizations and ind-

ividuals usually attend at no cost. Attendees of the presentation become eligible for the Ragins/Braswell National scholarship sponsored by Marianne. If you or your organization is interested in sponsoring a workshop or motivational presentation with Marianne Ragins, visit www.scholarshipworkshop.com.

The Scholarship Workshop Boot Camp

- This is an expanded version of The Scholarship Workshop presentation – It is a full day and a half of activities designed to help students and parents leave the weekend with scholarship essays, résumés, and applications completed and ready to go. The workshop boot camp is usually sponsored by various organizations and individuals usually attend at no cost. Attendees of the presentation become eligible for the Ragins/Braswell National scholarship sponsored by Marianne. If you or your organization is interested in sponsoring a workshop or motivational presentation with Marianne Ragins, visit www.scholarshipwork shop.com.

Webinars & Online Classes

- *The Scholarship Class for High School Students and Their Parents*

- *Scholarship, Fellowship & Grant Information Session for Students Already in College, Returning to College, and Pursuing Graduate School*
    - The above classes are webinar versions of the Scholarship Workshop presentation. It is offered for those who do not live in an area where a workshop is being sponsored. Attendees of either class become

eligible for the Ragins/Braswell National Scholarship.

- *Writing Scholarship & College Essays for the Uneasy Student Writer – A Webinar*

- *Turbocharge Your Résumé - Résumé Writing Skills to Help You Stand Out from the Crowd – A Webinar*

- *Preparation Skills for Scholarship & College Interviews – A Webinar*

- *Minimizing College Costs and Student Loans – A Webinar*

For more information about webinars and online classes available, visit www.scholarshipworkshop.com and see online classes.

eBooks

Marianne Ragins also has numerous e-Books available for Nook, Kindle and iPad. Visit www.scholarshipworkshop.com and see eBooks for the latest!

You can find information and additional resources from Marianne Ragins by visiting or connecting with her using the following:
- www.scholarshipworkshop.com
- www.facebook.com/scholarshipworkshop
- www.twitter.com/ScholarshipWork

About the Author

In her senior year of high school, Marianne Ragins won over $400,000 in scholarships for college. As perhaps the first student ever to amass nearly half a million dollars in scholarship money, she has been featured in many publications including *USA Today, People, Ebony, Newsweek, Money, Essence, Family Money, Black Enterprise* and on the cover of *Parade*. She has also made hundreds of radio and television appearances on shows such as "Good Morning America," "The Home Show," and the "Mike & Maty Show."

Marianne Ragins received a master of business administration (MBA) from George Washington University in Washington, DC and a bachelor of science (BS) degree in business administration from Florida Agricultural and Mechanical University in Tallahassee, Florida. Both degrees were entirely funded by scholarships and other free aid.

Marianne Ragins is also the author of the highly successful *Winning Scholarships for College: An Insider's Guide, College Survival & Success Skills 101* and many other publications. She is an experienced motivational speaker and lecturer who has traveled nationally and internationally conducting The Scholarship Workshop presentation and giving other motivational seminars and speeches. Marianne is the publisher of www.scholarshipworkshop.com, a scholarship and college information site, and sponsor of the *Leading the Future II* and *Ragins Braswell National Scholarships*.

Contact Marianne Ragins using any of the following sources:

- www.scholarshipworkshop.com
- www.facebook.com/scholarshipworkshop
- www.twitter.com/ScholarshipWork